Illustrated Lessons of Oboe, Music, and Life From Joe Robinson

Illustrated Lessons of Oboe, Music, And Life From Joe Robinson

by Oshri Hakak

Written and Illustrated by Oshri Hakak

Second Edition
Copyright © 2017, by Oshri Hakak
All Rights Reserved

Illustrated Lessons of Oboe, Music, and Life From Joe Robinson
Written and Illustrations by Oshri Hakak
ISBN: 978-0-692-89071-4

www.LivingInkFlow.com
Los Angeles

To Joe,

And to all
for whom the path

Is music

Forward

It was the end of a long and beautiful summer of traveling. The friendly dog, quiet house, and calm suburb of Chapel Hill, North Carolina, provided the perfect space for much needed quiet contemplation. I was house-and-dog-sitting for Joe Robinson, former Principal Oboist of the New York Philharmonic, and my oboe teacher for four years as an undergrad at Duke. He has also been an inspirational mentor, parental figure, and life guide.

Sneaking into his vacant home studio and sitting in the chair by his own, where I had always sat while he made reeds, taught music, and shared stories about his life and career, I remembered his open generosity and willingness to pass down everything he could— always crediting his own esteemed teachers. Life's path during and since then has taken me through work in behavioral neuroscience (studying time perception and prenatal nutrient supplementation), organizational psychology (for a small management consulting firm), international development (collecting textbooks, making mead, beekeeping), sales (for my brother-in-law's locksmith company), tutoring (most subjects K-8), teaching (social entrepreneurship, conflict mediation, business management), facilitating for Israeli-Palestinian dialogue forums, and performing on the oboe in Kirtan music for Kundalini Yoga classes.

Now working as an artist, musician, and teacher I see how Joe's lessons have helped me move throughout all of these stages (I am still involved in many of them), and how they have continually helped lead me towards more purpose, fulfillment, and happiness. He has been not just a great oboe teacher but a great life teacher. Sitting in his studio with my art supplies, I closed my eyes and remembered myself as a college student postured just as I was then, eagerly listening to soak up the wisdom of this man who brought his oboe playing from the Lenoir, NC, High School Band to the New York Philharmonic. The lessons flooded back to me over the days I spent in the peaceful home in Chapel Hill— lessons about how to play the oboe, how to create music, and how to live life.

A Note from Joe

"Almost every utterance you ascribe to me is derivative. There may not be a single original thought among them! It is only in nuances of expression and their particular assemblage that they may be considered authentic. Filial piety is at the heart of apprenticeship, which is our time-honored manner of learning and teaching applied music. I owe the greatest debt for everything in your collection of ideas to my own mentors----principally among them, John Mack, Marcel Tabuteau and Pablo Casals."

– Joe Robinson, 2013

*May these inks resonate with lasting benefit
for each person who gazes at them,
and may you hear the infinite
in just one note's vibration.*

Breathe through to your belly, not your chest, up there your lungs are trapped in a bony cage—

Don't over-prepare for your entrance — remember, the ball may enter your court at any point, so you need to stay flexible —

Just as you probably don't inhale before every time you speak, you don't need to inhale before every time you enter a phrase—

Just play the note!

Don't overanalyze—
sometimes we can be too smart for our own good—

Always

choose

an extraordinary experience

over

an ordinary one—

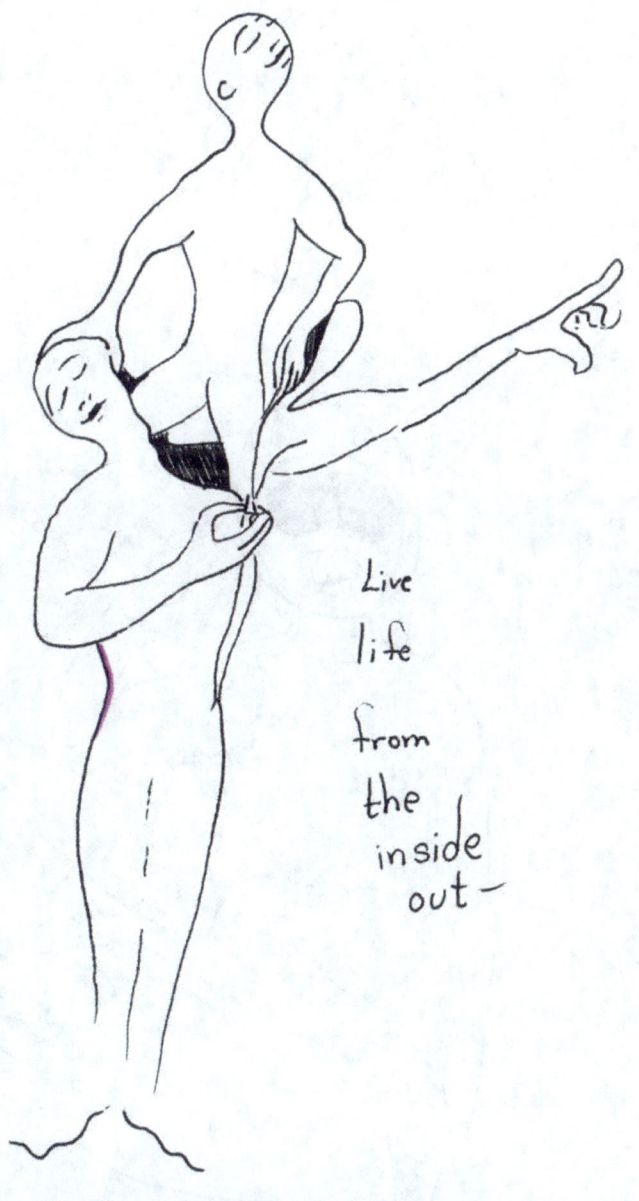

Once in a while,

stop
to play
a few notes
from the center—

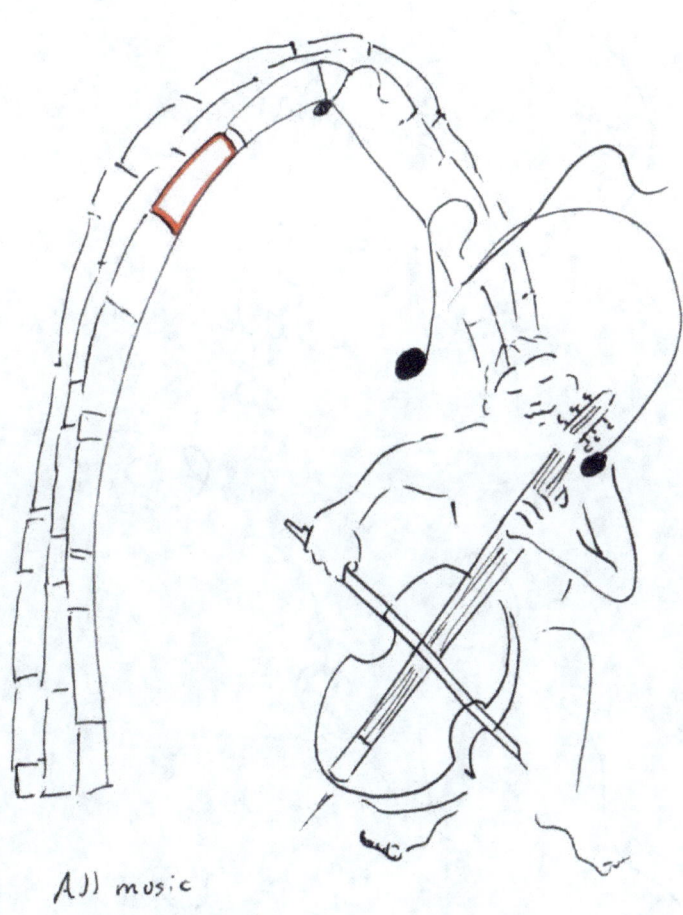

All music

is a series

of arches—

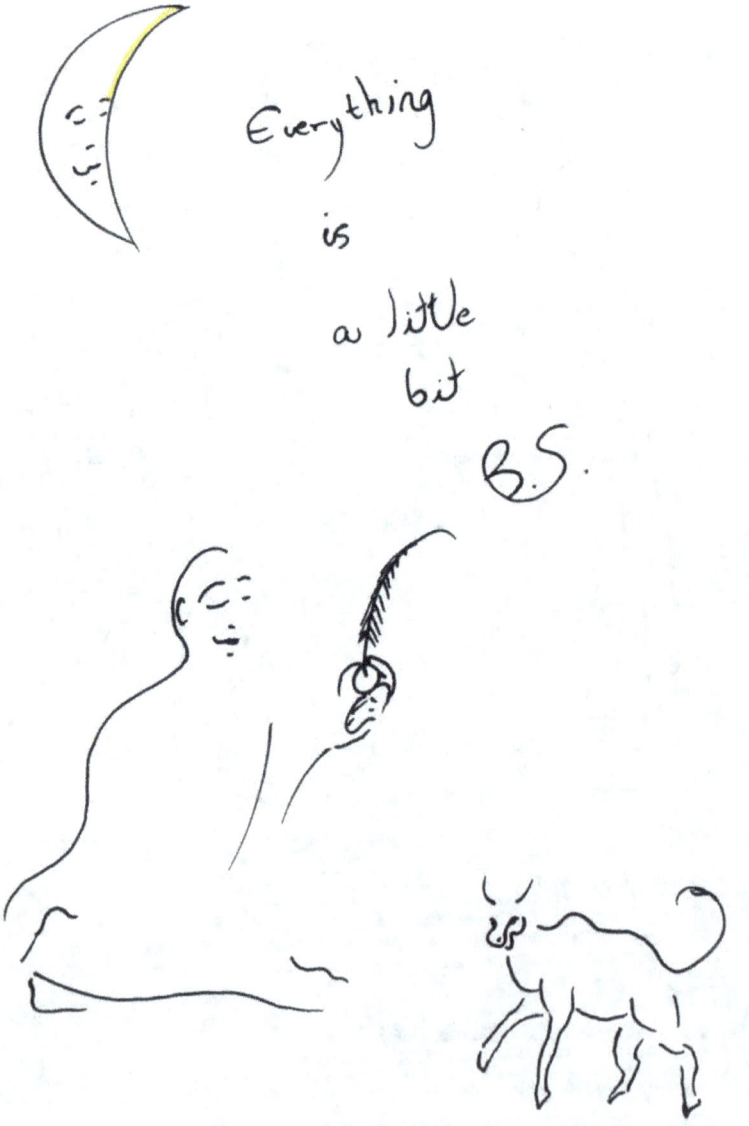

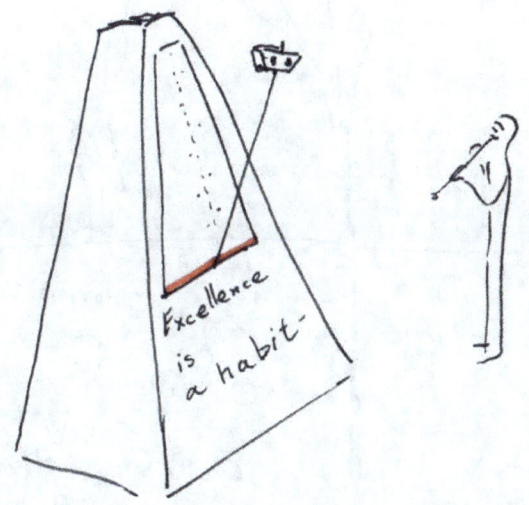

Good tone

is a matter
of life
and depth—

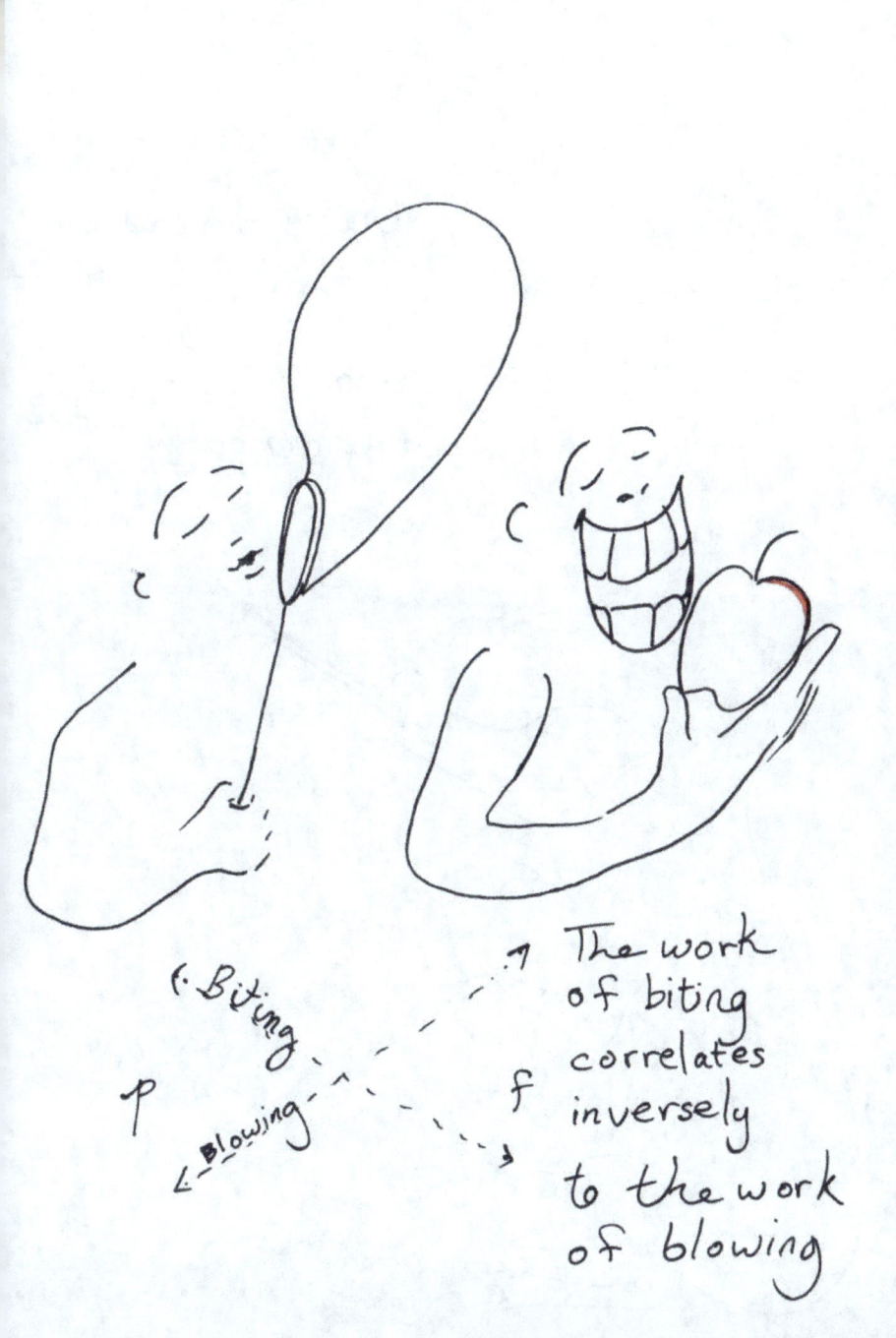

Keep
the embouchure
firm yet flexible—
avoid
the crocodile bite—

Say "oo"
for notes
in the
lower register,

and say "ee"
for notes
in the upper
register —

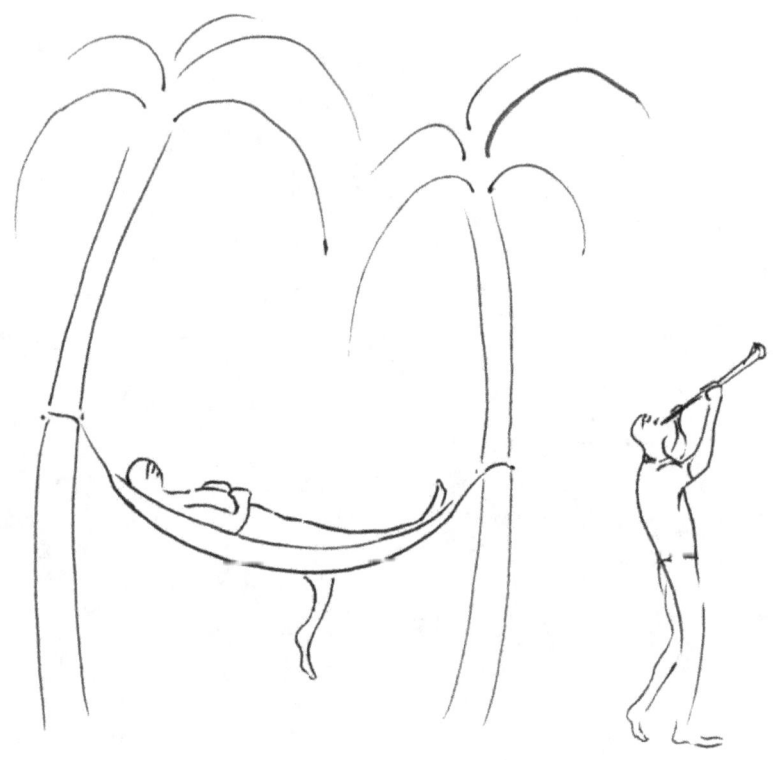

Sometimes
   a tiny adjustment
will mean the difference
between the frisbee
going 10 feet
and
100 yards —

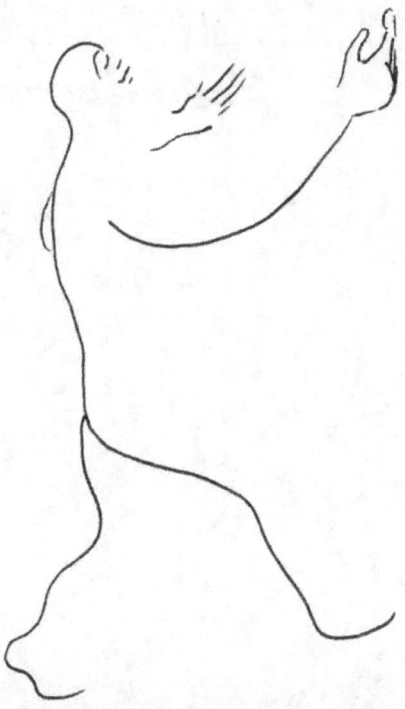

Remember
not all adjustments
apply
to all notes —

We can
analyze
wind production
day and night;

but
in the end
all that
matters
is what
happens
when your
air meets
the tip of
the reed—

the pressure
of the
wind against
the reed

should always
be present
even as
it adjusts,

like a
ping-pong
ball on
a fountain
of water—

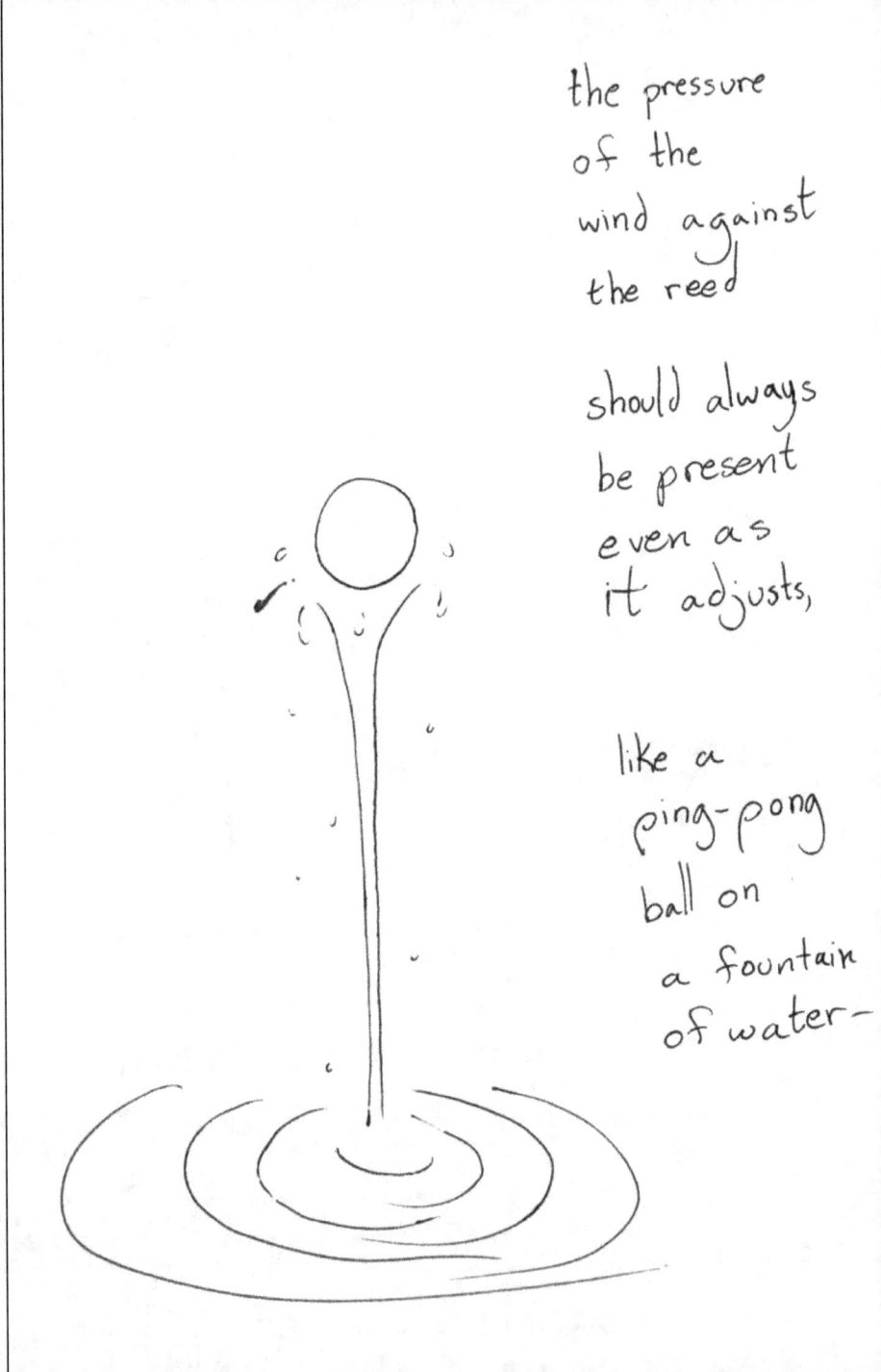

Spend time with the instrument to learn the individual feeling, the right kinesthetic pressure for each note —

It takes more air
to play loud than soft,
independent of the
constant opening-to-air
pressure ratio—

learn to laugh
hartily at yourself,
without
disparaging yourself —

The quintessential musical phrase

is depicted

perfectly

by the

shape of
the Pepperidge Farm
goldfish cracker

The solution
is often simply
more air—

let your fingers
on the keys

be as Prussian
soldiers—

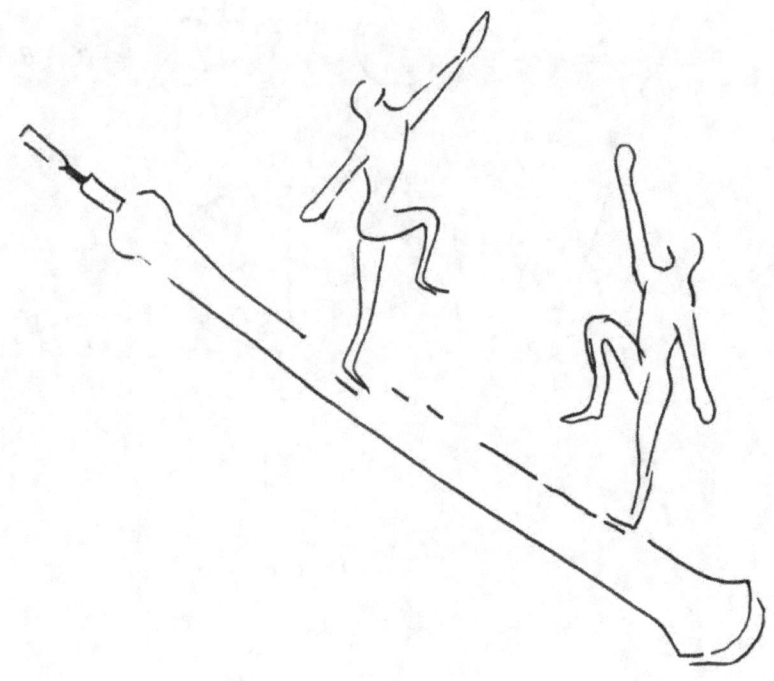

Develop your facility to go back and forth from ppp to fff both instantly and gradually, with ease —

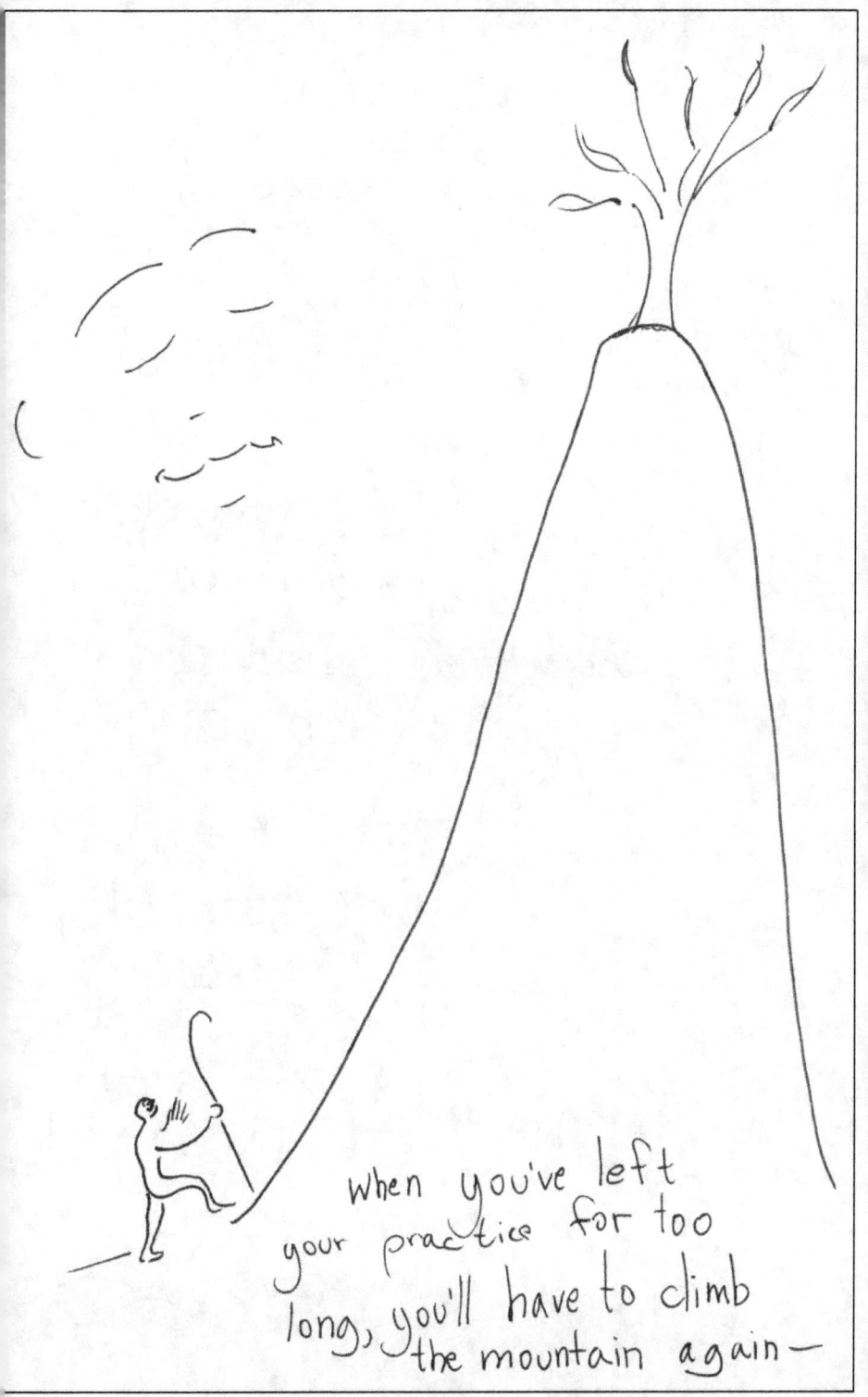

When you
find yourself

with only
a tiny bit of
time
   for your daily
    practice,
     use it
     to play

      ppp

       at the
        tip
         of
         the
         reed—

There are
many oysters
in the sea,
and only a few
who make pearls—
the teacher's job
is to provide
the irritant—

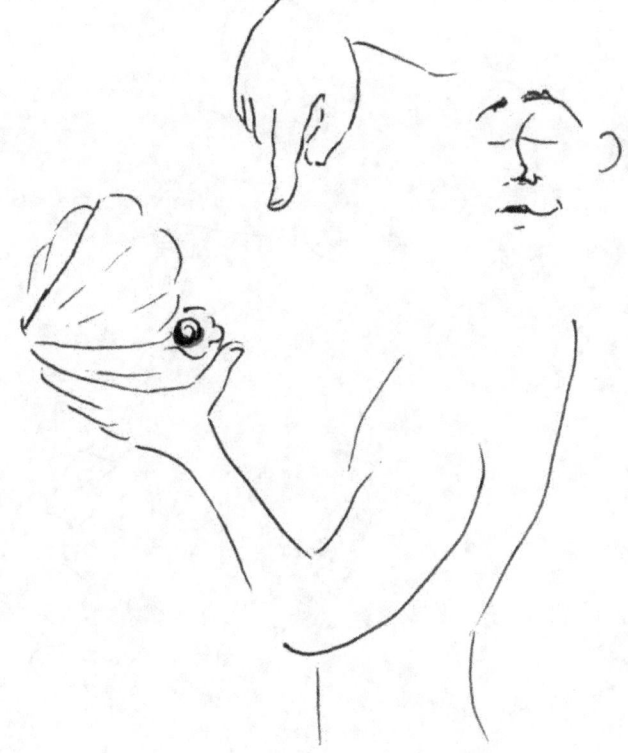

Keep the reed stretched in against your lips— at all times

In
a musical phrase,
you don't want
a horse to jump
and a dog
to land—

C
C
C

Remember to finish fully your phrases; it's nice of you to help an old woman across Park Avenue— but don't leave her stranded in the middle of the street

Embrace praise and applause — it's like mother's milk —

Some
of the hard
stuff may take
one hundred times
the practice
time
as some
of the easy
stuff
to get—

To the extent that you say or do anything meaningful, you will experience opposition—

time
is infinitely
abundant —
practice only
at the
speed of perfect
practice

or slower —

Take time
to find

your own
voice —

For all we know,

it's the
phase of
the moon
when
the cane
is plucked

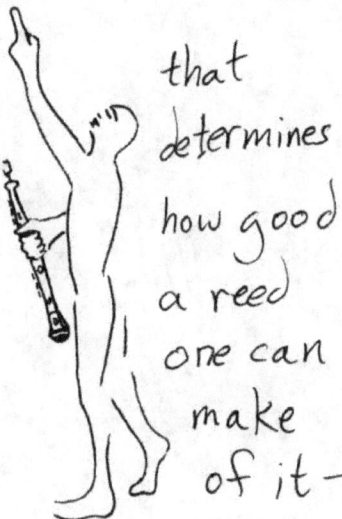

that
determines
how good
a reed
one can
make
of it —

Take risks,

but shed some fear of scar tissue, first—

all
kindness
has
intrinsic
value—

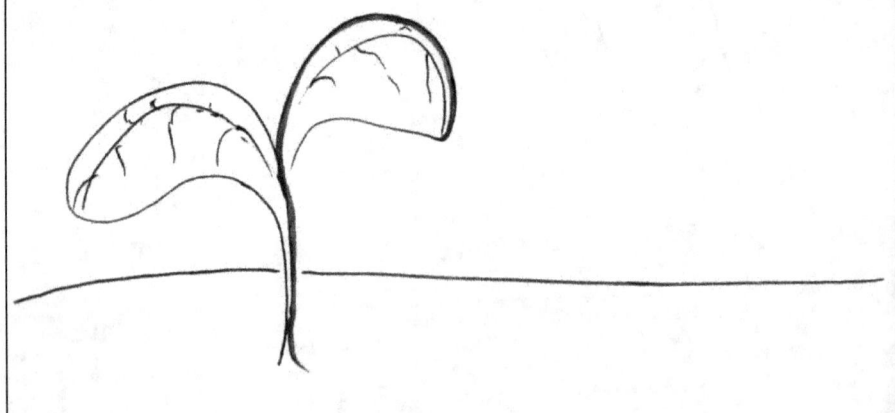

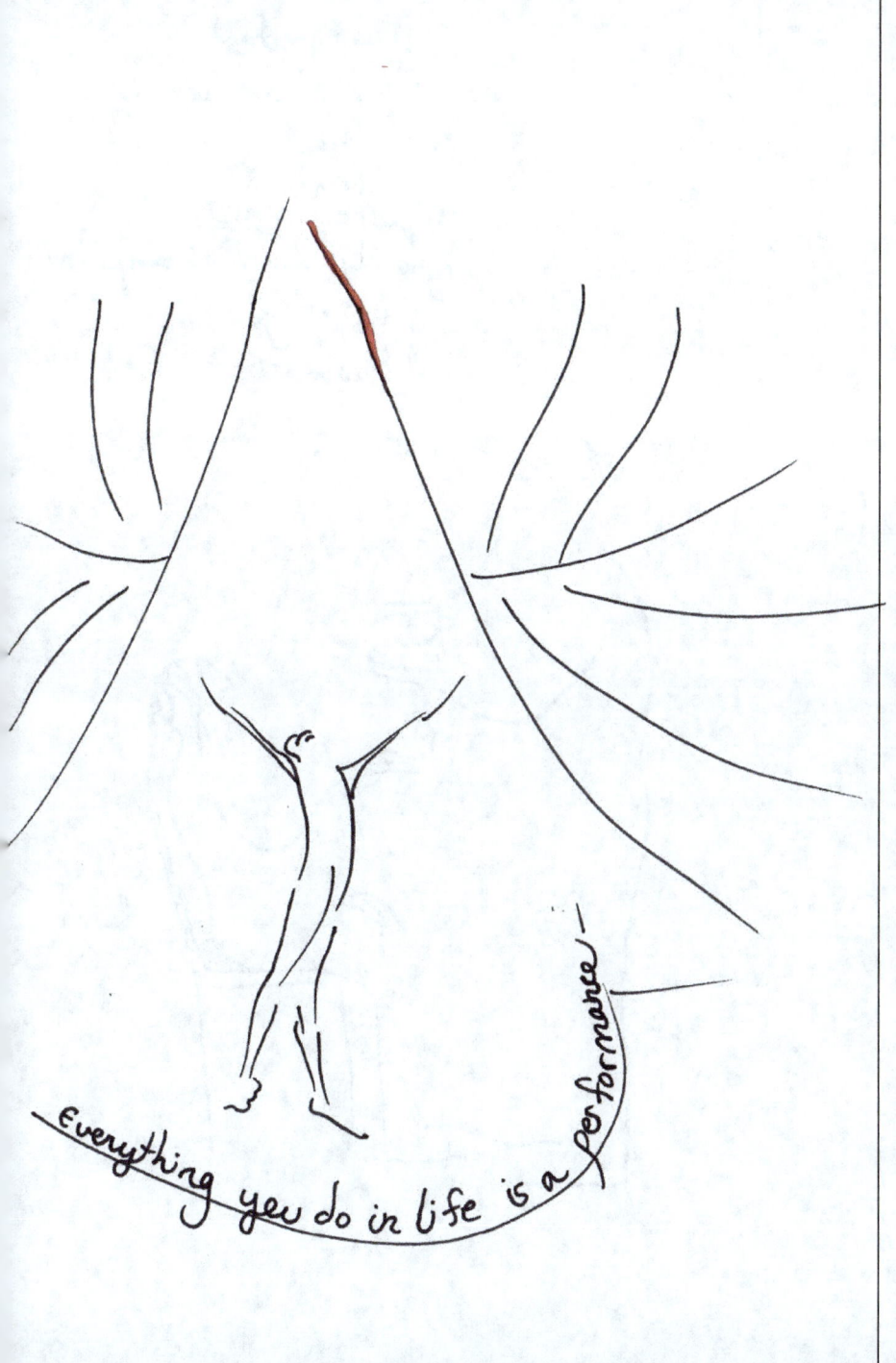

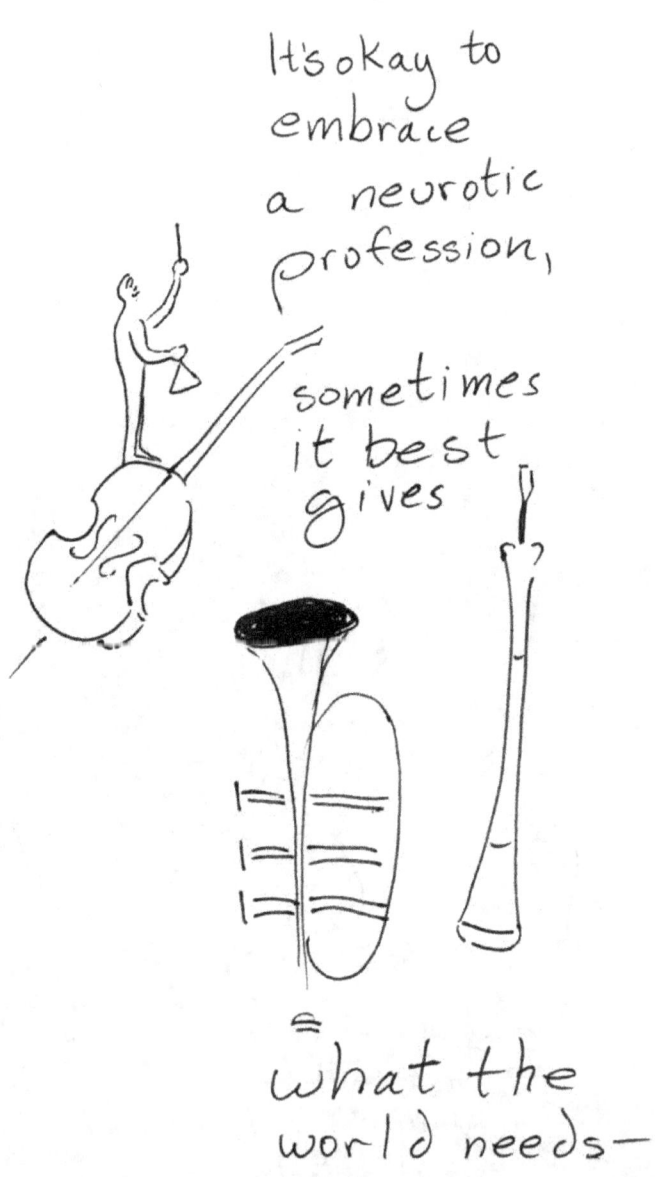

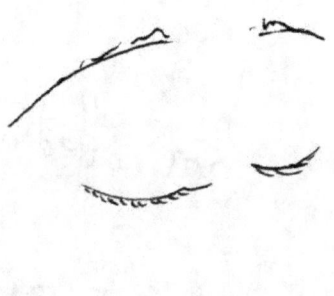

Practice
the
inner
work—

Spend time

practicing

controlled variation

of pitch

and dynamic

using
just
the
reed—

Anyone who's anyone is an amalgam-

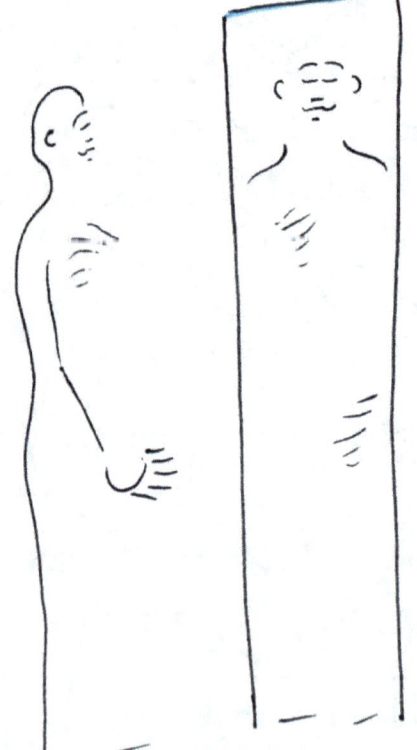

The goal of every great teacher is for the student to go further than the teacher—

Accept the gems from your teacher and pass them on —

To see more of Oshri Hakak's artwork, visit:

www.LivingInkFlow.com

or find him on Instagram at @oshrihakak

www.ingramcontent.com/pod-product-compliance
Lightning Source LLC
Chambersburg PA
CBHW070528010526
44110CB00050B/2270